GREAT Pets

ADULT COLORING BOOK

PRAISE MY PET!

WWW.PRAISEMYPET.COM

COLOR JACKIE AND MIMI!

4

COLOR JACKIE AND MIMI!

4

COLOR FAUCHY AND CHACO!

5

COLOR SHELBY AND MARBLE!

7

COLOR SYLVIE AND ANGELINA!

9

COLOR RORY GILMORE AND REVELSTOKE!

COLOR JAMES AND MAX!

15

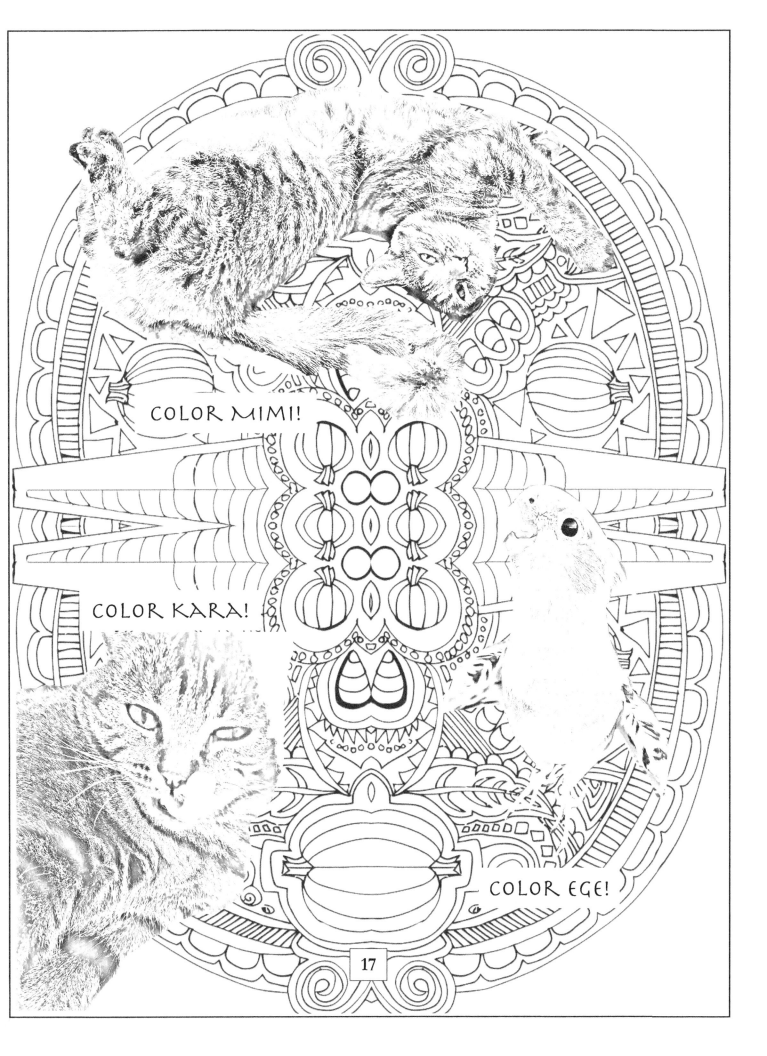

COLOR ROCKY, CHARRITO, JOTARO AND AMANDA!

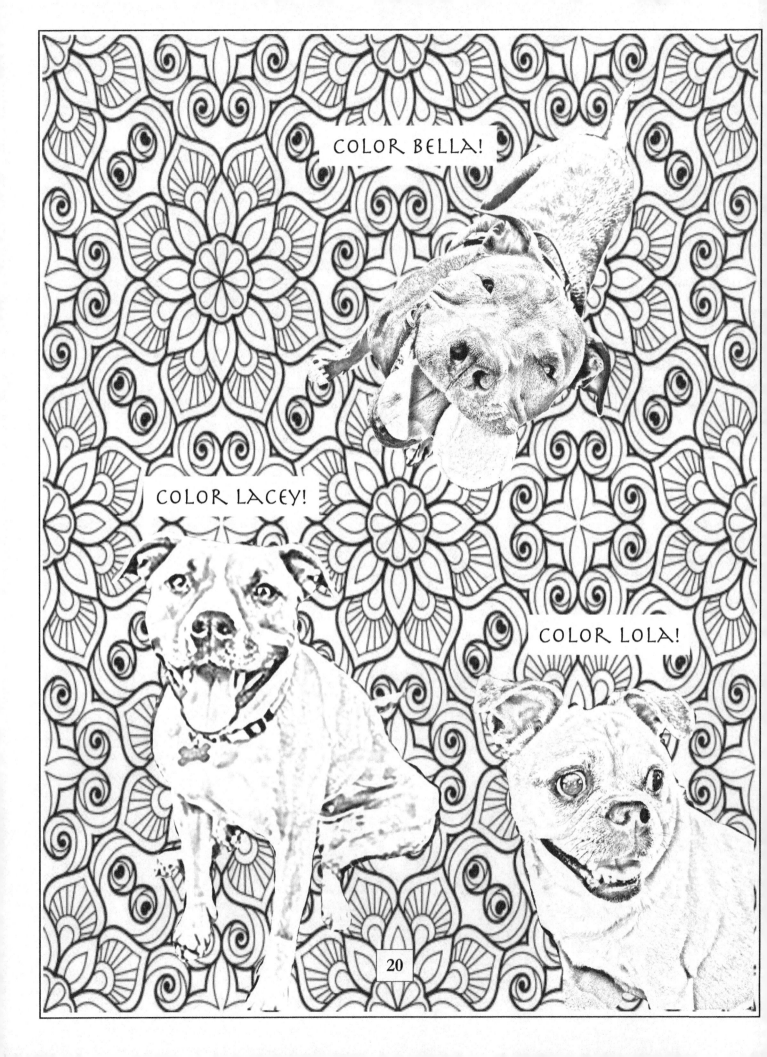

COLOR ME-ME AND GRACIE!

21

COLOR SNOW AND COSTA!

23

COLOR HUTCH!

COLOR LUCAS!

27

COLOR CAESAR!

COLOR CORBEN AND BOB!

36

COLOR BUFF AND CABEZA!

37

COLOR CHUY, BRUCE, SID AND GUS!

39

COLOR HONEY BUN AND DAISY!

41

COLOR NACHO AND LUNA!

COLOR OPIE, JAX AND LUCY!

44

COLOR SYDNEY AND DARWIN!

49

COLOR PADDINGTON!

COLOR ALFIE!

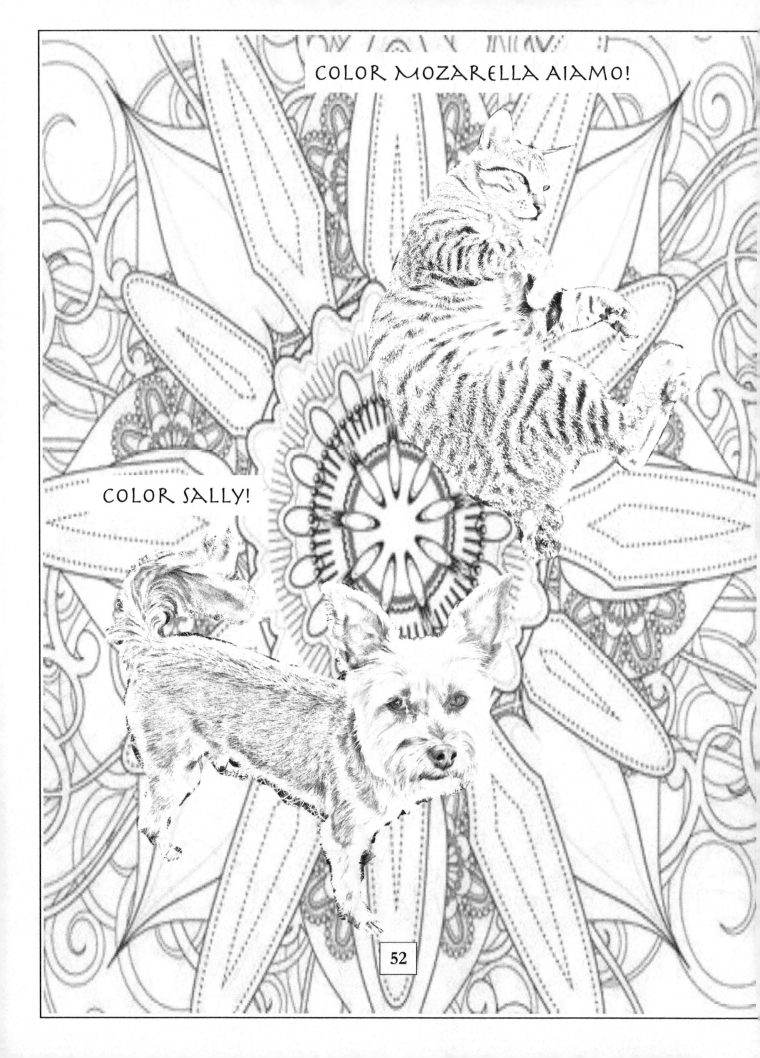

COLOR MOZARELLA AIAMO!

COLOR SALLY!

52

53

COLOR ESSY, MINNY AND LUKE!

54

COLOR GRACIE!

COLOR ROSIE!

COLOR KOSSEI!

56

COLOR THE POTCAKE/SHIH TZU!

COLOR JASPER!

COLOR BISCUIT!

COLOR EDDIE AND RUSTY!

59

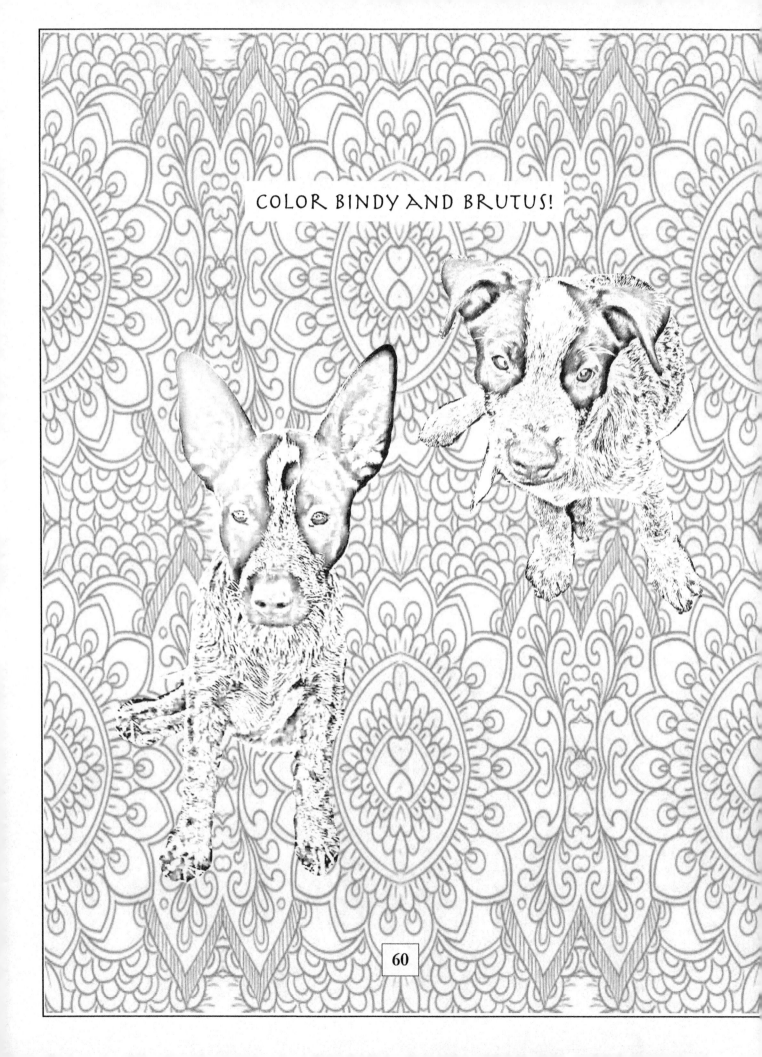

COLOR BINDY AND BRUTUS!

60

COLOR BELLA!

COLOR THOR!

COLOR VEGAS!

61

COLOR SIMON STANLEY, LITTLE BIT AND PEPPERONI!

COLOR BOSS AND PETE!

63

COLOR TERIYAKI BRUNO!

COLOR SAMSON!

COLOR DICE!

64

COLOR XIAOMI!

COLOR JERRY!

COLOR BAGEL!

COLOR BACON, NINA AND HEIDI!

69

71

COLOR HAZEL AND FLASH!

COLOR LOKI AND RONNIE!

73

COLOR KADER!

COLOR HUXLEY!

77

COLOR LARRY AND MEEKO!

83

COLOR BOSCO, BORIS, AND NOBLE!

COLOR YOKO AND MOMO!

85

COLOR SKY!

COLOR THE CAT!

88

COLOR TRIGGER AND HUNTER!

90

COLOR KUDZU!

COLOR PIPER!

COLOR DESTINY, GINGER, FAITH, NUGGET, COOKIE, CAPPUCCINO AND VANILLA!

COLOR ATHENA AND SASHA JAYDAVINE!

COLOR DAPHNE!

COLOR BEAR!

95

COLOR THOR!

COLOR BETSY!

COLOR B!

97

COLOR APOLLO AND ECLIPSE!

99

We hope you enjoyed our coloring book! If you'd like to see YOUR pet in one of our upcoming coloring books, visit www.praisemypet.com/pages/send-us-your-pet-photos

Happy coloring!

Made in the USA
Monee, IL
18 December 2020